Also by Cheri Huber

From A Center for the Practice of Zen Buddhist Meditation
Time-Out for Parents: A Compassionate Approach to Parenting*
The Monastery Cookbook: Low-fat Vegetarian recipes

From Keep It Simple Books
The Key and the Name of the Key Is Willingness*
How You Do Anything Is How You Do Everything: A Workbook
There Is Nothing Wrong With You: Going Beyond Self-Hate*
The Depression Book: Depression as an Opportunity for Spiritual Growth, 2nd Ed.
The Fear Book: Facing Fear Once and for All*
Nothing Happens Next: Responses to Questions about Meditation
Be the Person You Want to Find: Relationship and Self-Discovery*
Sex and Money...are dirty, aren't they? A Guided Journal
Suffering Is Optional: Three Keys to Freedom and Joy

From Present Perfect Books (Sara Jenkins, editor)
Trying to Be Human: Zen Talks from Cheri Huber*
Turning Toward Happiness: Conversations with a Zen Teacher and Her Students
Good Life: A Zen Precepts Retreat with Cheri Huber
Buddha Facing the Wall: Interviews with American Zen Monks
Sweet Zen: Dharma Talks with Cheri Huber

*Videotapes from Openings***
There Are No Secrets: Zen Meditation with Cheri Huber
Yoga for Meditators *with Christa Rypins*
Yoga for A Better Back *with Christa Rypins and Dr. John Sousa*
Yummy Yoga: Stress Relief for Hips, Back, and Neck *with Christa Rypins*

*Audiotape from Who's Here? Productions***
Getting Started Going Deeper: Introduction to Meditation

*Available as a book on tape from Keep It Simple
**Also available from Keep It Simple
Please see the order form at the end of this book.
All items except books on tape are available through your local bookstore.

THAT WHICH YOU ARE SEEKING IS CAUSING YOU TO SEEK

INCLUDES "ONE LESS ACT OF VIOLENCE"

Cover design by Mary Denkinger
Cover art by Sharon Williams

DEDICATION

This book is dedicated to the memory of Sylvia Elizabeth Reid (May 11, 1944 — January 19, 1989).

In April, 1988, Sylvia discovered an enlarged lymph node under her left arm. The doctor didn't even send it to the lab, it was so obviously malignant. Sylvia began in earnest the work of completing her life.

I asked her at one point how she wanted her life to be. She said that if this were to be the last year of her life, she wanted to devote herself completely to her practice. She had always wanted to write but felt that until she found Buddhism there was nothing to write about. Now she wanted to write about this practice, for herself and with the hope that others might find it helpful.

There are some standard questions that arise when people read our first book, The Key, and Sylvia set about the task of trying to answer them. (Pages 1, 17, 21, 29, 42, 56, 71, 77, 92, 100, 104)

In September, the cancer spread to her lungs and much of the writing fell away. She still continued to meet with people from our meditation group, willing to share all she was learning from her process of letting go of life. It wasn't necessarily that she felt that she had written all she wanted to write, it was more that she wanted her attention to be with her moment by moment experience and writing felt extra.

For a while we meditated with her in her home rather than at the Zen Center, and she shared her wisdom and clarity with the Sangha until a few days before her death.

She died January 19, 1989. Her final words were, "It's been nothing but wonderful," her final voluntary movement, gasshō. And so in deep gasshō, our hearts filled with love and gratitude, we dedicate this book to Sylvia.

INTRODUCTION

If we didn't already know the experience of
what we're looking for, we would never look.
It simply would not occur to us. The Buddha
left wife, son, wealth, power, and privi-
lege because intuitively he knew that
there must be something that would make
sense out of what appears to be the
senseless, useless suffering that life brings.
We remain dissatisfied (suffering) as long
as we are identified with an illusion of
separateness. We know we are separate,
but separate from what? We feel alone,
isolated, abandoned — but what are we
missing? What have we lost?

We begin to seek — where, what is that
which we long for, our essence, our True
Nature, that which we truly are? — and
slowly, painstakingly we begin to follow
it home. Haltingly, fearfully, sometimes
excitedly, joyfully, we begin to follow it
back to itself, back to who we really
are.

What we are looking for is causing us
to look. That's why we need not go
anywhere, do anything, learn more,

figure it out, worry about going wrong. We need only stop, sit down, be still, and pay attention.

We feel this simple little book will assist you in doing just that.

In loving kindness,

Cheri

ACKNOWLEDGMENTS

In 1984, I was struggling with one of countless revisions of a "manuscript" which I fervently hoped would one day become a book about spiritual practice as we do it. I continued to get to the same point of "but I'm just not a writer" and yet remained committed to the task. Many assisted me through that long process, giving feedback and encouragement. But it only truly took form and became what I consider to be the excellent representation of and introduction to our practice which The Key and the Name of the Key Is Willingness is when it was passed into the capable, creative, wise, and talented head, heart, and hands of June Shiver.

In 1987, I handed over a couple of hundred thoughts and questions that had come up through several years of workshops to Sylvia and June who turned them into the How You Do Anything Is How You Do Everything workbook. Sylvia contributed much to order and direction, June added continuity, design, and illustrations, and filled in all the gaps.

After Sylvia's death, June began the task of turning what Sylvia had written (see Dedication) into the sequel that Sylvia had hoped it would be. Her patience and dedication have been limitless. Much of the text she has written herself, much she has edited from talks by the guide and workshops at the Zen Center.

I would especially like to express appreciation to the Sangha for the depth of their commitment to this practice.

I wrote "One Less Act of Violence" and included it in this book because for me it is the practical application of our spiritual practice. Ours is a practice of ending suffering. It seems to me that it is impossible to end suffering while practicing violence on any level.

Many thanks to Jeanne DuPrau for lending her myriad talents to the preparation of "One Less Act of Violence".

FOREWORD

This book isn't organized in any particular order, but then life isn't organized in any particular order. Life startles us because we keep falling asleep, and if we're asleep, if we're not present, of course we're going to be startled. We're going along feeling like we've sort of got the hang of something and, oops! a sudden curve. This book reads like that, and that's all right because we need to be reminded to pay attention. Each moment is new and full of possibilities so how can we expect to know anything about it if we're dozing?

It's good not to be lulled into a false sense of security and stability. We like things to be consistent and predictable so that our sleep won't be disturbed.

◆ ◆ ◆ ◆   In spiritual practice it's good to be disturbed. We want to be disturbed as long as we can be disturbed. When you are not disturbed it's only because you are not disturbed, not because nothing is disturbing. It is true that nothing is intrinsically disturbing, but as long as you can be disturbed, you can't know that. So if we want to wake up, if we want to see how we create disturbance and suffering within ourselves, we will want to continue to be disturbed and to pay very close attention to being disturbed for as long as we are disturbed!

If you can read that and smile, you're ready to go on with this book and you'll probably enjoy it. If you read that and find nothing to smile about, you're ready to go on with this book — it just probably won't be as much fun. In either case, see if you can open your heart and mind and approach this book one moment at a time.

"Overcome evil with good,
     and falsehood with truth,
          and hatred with love."

This is the message Peace Pilgrim used to carry, a message we've been hearing since the beginning of recorded history. She would often remind us of that, emphasizing that there was nothing new in what she said, only in what she did, which was to live that message. We've all heard it a million times. Why say it again? Don't we already know these things?

Yes, we know the words, but most of us are still struggling to live them. And if saying them again will help someone in that struggle, then the message is worth repeating. We offer this book in that spirit — not because it says anything new, but because it points us toward the doing, being, and living. It is the practice behind the words that interests us.

Of course, the practice isn't new either. We have all lived the meaning behind the words — a few throughout entire lifetimes, others only now and

1

then. But even if it has been done before, when we are truly living this practice, when our awareness and the present moment are one, we are infinitely new — infinitely new in our willingness, acceptance, wisdom, love, and compassion; infinitely new in who we really are and who we've always been.

Most people's lives are
salvage operations...

never going back to adequacy,
never going back to that place of
peace and plenty.

In our practice...

it is not what we do, it is how we do
not what we think, but how we think
not what we feel, but how we feel.

This is a very important aspect of our
teaching. In this way we learn to take full
responsibility for ourselves. We can never
blame another for our actions or reactions.

We feel our own feelings. We pay lip service to the pain of others, but the fact is <u>we</u> <u>can't</u> <u>feel</u> it. My neighbor's broken leg is not as painful to me as the broken date I really wanted to go on. People and animals are dying horrible deaths everywhere, but pain for me is not getting the job I want, or having my car break down, or having my lover leave me for someone else.

No one is doing anything to us. Being left, ignored, or abandoned is an awful feeling — except when we're left, ignored, or abandoned by someone we dislike. Then it's heaven.

Our problems, our concerns, our emotions are our own. When we feel them, they're ours and they're "real"; when we don't, they hardly exist.

The answers we are seeking are ever present. We are never unconscious, we are never unaware, we are often inattentive.

Nothing is hidden.

All we want to know is available in each moment. We become more attentive by being more willing.

One wants to wake up. Suffering has ceased to be interesting. There has been a huge loss or failure or disappointment. Perhaps there is simply an awareness that life is not working, that life as it is and has been is not satisfactory.

So One begins to look. One begins to question. After a time One considers a meditation practice as a way to see more clearly. One seeks instruction and One begins to sit.

In the beginning One enjoys sitting. "This is great. This is interesting. This feels right." However, before long, ego, that illusion of separateness which you call I, me, my says, "This is too much!"

I hates this! I is not having a good time. I doesn't want to sit still. I doesn't want to be aware. I doesn't want to be observed, scrutinized. I wants to be free (not free of suffering, not enlightened—although that would be okay if I doesn't need to change in order to get it), I wants to be free to do what I wants when I wants to do it.

Yet when I is thus "free", I suffers.

"I don't want to suffer," says I.

"Yet what you do leads to suffering," One replies.

"It's not my fault," says I.

"It's not a matter of fault," One replies, "it's a matter of feeling inadequate."

"Are you saying I'm inadequate?"

"No, just suggesting that you might think you are."

"I do what I have to do," defends I.

"Is that enough?" asks One.

"Not usually," admits I, "It seems that as soon as I satisfy one need or want, there's another right behind."

"Could you consider another way?" asks One.

"I am afraid," says I.

Sit down in a comfortable position that enables you to keep your back straight. Relax your abdomen, drop your shoulders. Let your eyes rest 3 or 4 feet in front of you. Take a few deep breaths and then let your breathing return to normal.

Feel your body breathing. Feel the air enter your body, fill your body, and leave your body.

Thoughts will arise and pass away. Feelings will arise and pass away. You may hear sounds, smell odors, see sights, feel sensations. Just notice them, resisting nothing, holding onto nothing (resisting no thing, holding onto no thing), allowing everything to be as it is.

Just sit- not trying to accomplish anything, not trying to change anything, especially yourself. Breathe in and breathe out.

Aware   Right here
Alert   Right now
Attentive   Accepting what is
Present   Simply noticing

We are always willing.
We have all the willingness we need.
We just have to look at what we're willing for.

If we want to be free, we must be willing to be free of our beliefs,
        of our better ideas,
        of our self-rejection,
        of our resistance to what is.

For instance, if I have a better idea about how I <u>should</u> be (more compassionate toward others) and I go through a process of rejecting myself every time I don't meet my standards, I will <u>never</u> find that compassion. The essential thing I have forgotten here is

ONE PROCESS
    DOES NOT LEAD
        TO ANOTHER.

Rejection does not lead to compassion.
Compassion leads to compassion.
Rejection leads to rejection.

If you see something you don't like about the way you are

and you beat yourself up for it, pretty soon you will have trained yourself to stop looking.

Congratulate yourself whenever you see something hard. It means you're growing.

You need pencil and paper for this one.

1) List three character traits which you consider undesivable.

2) Own those traits. Allow yourself to see how you exhibit each one. Write it down.

3) See if you can in no way, on any level, disapprove of yourself for having those traits. To do this you must give yourself unconditional love and acceptance. (Oh, go ahead. Risk it.)

We often approach ourselves with ideas about improving, changing, or getting rid of various aspects. We are so conditioned to loss and deprivation that we automatically think of "disciplining" ourselves as "depriving" ourselves.

Let's not get rid of, let's add. Instead of stopping eating, let's add exercise.

It's easy to love ourselves when we're being good and meeting our standards. The practice is to love ourselves when we've not.

Everytime you do something you disapprove of, instead of beating yourself — "I shouldn't have done that" "I should change" "I always say the wrong thing"— open your heart to compassion. This is the only "change" you need. After all, it's the parts of ourselves who are suffering who need our unconditional love.

"But how can I become a good person without disciplining myself?"

Remember, one process does not lead to another. Punishment does not lead to love. There is no "good person" outside of compassion. When we truly know this, when in the deepest part of our heart we find that compassion, we won't continue to disappoint ourselves.

One of the most basic beliefs we hold is that there is something wrong with us. We believe we're bad, inadequate, lacking. We must find the courage to prove to ourselves that inherently we are goodness.

Disciplining ourselves, rejecting ourselves, beating ourselves leads us farther away from this goodness, not closer to it.

FIRST STEP: not to punish ourselves because we're afraid we'll be bad
SECOND STEP: not beating ourselves when we don't meet our standards
THIRD STEP: having the patience and courage to examine those standards (Are they true? Does the process of reward and punishment work? etc.)

In this practice we don't punish people - internal or external - because they don't meet our standards or because they don't do what we want them to do.

The practice is finding compassion no matter what.

Assume:
   that there is a broader picture than your own point of view.

Risk:
   that if you let go of your egocentric investment in maintaining your point of view, you might get a glimpse of what that broader picture is.

Trust:
   that there is a good chance you'll even like what you see.

Pain and suffering. We often hear the words together — so often that, in common usage, their meanings have become synonymous. But from the perspective of this practice, they are quite different.

Pain is inevitable, a fact of life. There isn't a creature alive who hasn't experienced some kind of pain sometime and will live to experience it again — whether it's physical, psychological, or emotional. We know we can count on it, and yet we spend most of our time trying to prevent it.

Pain is not suffering. Suffering is our reaction to pain. Defensiveness, greed, anger, denial, repression, rejection, hatred, fear — to name a few — are all, at their source, reactions to pain — ego's reaction to pain. Ego takes pain very personally — pain reinforces its sense of separateness. Pain is a "something" to be gotten rid of or prevented. "I don't want this pain," "Get rid of this," "Something's wrong with me," "This shouldn't be happening" — are all things ego might say during a painful experience. Ego takes pain and adds suffering to it until the two are so intertwined that it's easy to see why we take the two words to mean the same thing.

The suffering we add to pain is often after the fact. I have a painful experience, then I try to figure out how I can arrange my life so that I don't experience that pain again. I am willing to make sacrifices for security, for control. For instance, I might stay with work I hate because I'm afraid of not being able to find something else, or afraid of being dependent— both painful experiences. Or having experienced the pain of an unrequited love, I now say good-bye to lovers before they can say good-bye to me.

We suffer when we are not willing to feel pain. We close ourselves off. We dig trenches. We put up barricades. We develop "sensitive" radar systems. And when provoked, we attack. All because we don't want to feel pain. All because pain frightens ego. Ego is vulnerable in its presence — vulnerable to being found out. Because when we stay with pain and don't add ego's suffering to it by closing ourselves off, we see that we are in fact equal to that pain, that we can "take it"; we see through ego's game of inadequacy. We see the wholeness and truth of our essential being. And we see that, like every-thing else, no one pain lasts forever.

I have lost my favorite teacup.
I have two choices.

I can have lost my
teacup and be
miserable.

I can have lost my
teacup and be
all right.

In either case, the teacup is gone.

"What is ego?"

The illusion that I am separate from everything else. The part of me who's always comparing, the part who feels superior, or inadequate, or deprived. It is the one who clings and resists, who sees me as subject and everything else as object. It is the source of my suffering.

"Why is it an illusion? You _are_ separate, aren't you? How can you be more than what you are? You're a person — and a very specific one at that. You're not your Uncle Bob. You're not a cat, a tree, a rock, and everything else that is. You are you."

Yes, I am me, but what animates me is what animates Uncle Bob, the cat, the tree, the rock, and all that is. We are packaged differently, but we share the same essence. There are many of us and we are not the same, but we are all one.

"How did this illusion of separateness

get started?"

Perhaps we bring it with us at birth or are just born with the capacity to develop it, and as we grow older, it is reinforced through years of conditioning. Maybe the reason we're here in the first place is to become aware of it so that we can let go of it.

"But if we're born with it, doesn't that mean it's good, that it's natural? Why should we get rid of it?"

It is not a matter of "should" or "good" or "getting rid of." It is a matter of ending our suffering. When we are ready to do that, we will.

The degree to which I am proud /
delighted / smug when I am "right"
is the degree to which I will suffer
when I am "wrong."

If I don't need to take credit,
I don't need to take blame.

When we are
- identified with a separate self who
  suffers
- seeking better accommodation
- trying to get what we want
- seeing the world in terms of I-me-my
we are coming from
- an assumption of inadequacy
- a feeling of being "other than"
- a feeling of being separate
- seeing self as subject and everything
  else as object.

When we turn away from our Heart,
from our True Nature, we feel unequal,
one-down. Seeking better accommodation,
trying to get what we want, comes
from an assumption that we don't have
enough as we are. We have to strive
constantly to do more, be more, get
more in order to feel equal to life.
   We say, "I want to be happy and free.
I don't choose to suffer. I don't choose
to feel inadequate." In order for us
to know our Adequacy, we must be
willing to examine closely our egos, our
conditioned minds. The reason we aren't
is because that very examination results
in a loss of identity. Ego prefers to

feel inadequate as an excuse to cling to its clear-cut, safe, self-imposed boundaries. Ego, I, sees scrutiny as death. I dies, and I does not want to do that. I would rather exist and struggle and suffer than experience itself as dying in order for there to be an identification with Adequacy.

We would not die if we switched from an identification with separateness to That Which Contains separateness. It's only the I that experiences itself as no longer existing. This is because I is no longer perceived as the center of the universe, which it is when we identify with egocentricity.

The bind we are caught in is choosing something that is suffering and then trying not to suffer within that. It's endless frustration and disappointment and futility and there is no alternative, unless we choose to let go of an egocentric life.

"Letting go"
does not mean
"not having."

although egocentricity thinks it does . . .

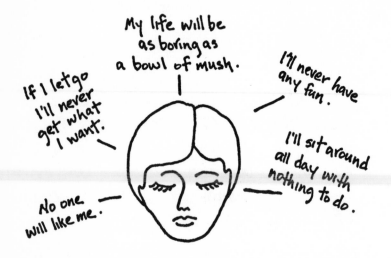

My life will be
as boring as
a bowl of mush.

If I let go
I'll never
get what
I want.

I'll never have
any fun.

I'll sit around
all day with
nothing to do.

No one
will like me.

We let go of our <u>attachment to getting</u> what we want. We aren't required to let go of the "what", the object of our desire.

And if we let go of that attachment, the odds of getting what we want will be just as good as ever. The only real difference will be that we won't suffer if we don't get it.

What if you could be
as happy as you can be

and not be getting what you want?

Joy is not the product of
getting what you want...

Joy is compassion turned inward—
the end of struggle,
the end of competition.

"What makes us do something we know will make us miserable? It seems that we choose to suffer."

We see ourselves going down the same roads over and over again. We begin to see that they lead to suffering, and yet we continue to choose them almost as if we didn't know how to do anything else. Every time I overeat, I feel sick and hate myself. Every time I fall in love, the object of my affection rejects or betrays me. Every time I feel depressed, I go on a buying binge and regret it later.

It's important to know that the problem or suffering is not in the overeating and feeling sick, the falling in love, or the depression. The trouble starts when I beat on myself for overeating, bewail my fate for falling in love with someone who doesn't love me, and feel guilty for buying things I don't need. The suffering is in my response to what is. I don't like what is. I would like it to change even though "what is" is now "what was" and can't change. Why do I torture myself like this?

I begin to suspect a pay-off. Would I find myself in the same fix over and over again if I didn't get something out of it? Probably not. So what is this pay-off? The pay-off is in knowing who I am as a familiar, separate self. I am gluttonous. I am unlovable. I am self-indulgent. But most important of all, I am separate. Ego is my identification with separateness, and I experience this separateness when I resist what is.

"So we suffer because we have egos? If we are born with egos, does that mean we are meant to suffer and that we can't change?"

Ego is the _process_ of our suffering. It is a how, not a what. When we understand how we do something, we are free to change it.

It's both sad and funny — something happens to me and I get hurt. I spend most of my life tensed against that experience and it's already over, it already happened and it's never going to happen again.

But something else will.

I'm focused on the past and something in the present snags me. I shift my attention to that, now also in the past, and I bump into something else in the present.

I'm always protecting myself from the experience I just had!

Don't miss
→ now ←
for
← then →

Always do
→ now ←
for
NOW

Then when
← then →
is
→ now ←

You will still
be doing
NOW
for*
N☸W

* EIGHT- SPOKED WHEEL— SYMBOL OF THE BUDDHA'S
EIGHT-FOLD PATH FOR ENDING SUFFERING

get current.

Make sure you're not still carrying around old ideas about yourself that aren't really applicable to your present life...

... and perhaps never were!

"The Jar"
- allow about 10 minutes -

Sit or lie in a comfortable position. Breathe slowly and easily. Close your eyes. After a few minutes, picture a jar in front of you. The purpose of the jar is to hold your thoughts. Take each thought as it comes to you and put it in the jar. Watch closely and each time you recognize a thought, put it in the jar...

Now take one thought out and concentrate on it for a moment.

Check in after a bit to see if you're still concentrating on that thought.

Now put it back in the jar with the others and see if you can let them all go for a moment, knowing that you can go back and think about any of them at some other time.

When we're present we are equal to life. It's the belief that we need to be afraid and protect ourselves that keeps us stuck. That belief isn't based on anything and it's not protecting us from anything.

"Yes, but, to some extent protecting ourselves is survival. If we didn't do that we wouldn't learn not to step in front of a moving car, for instance."

It seems that way except have you ever been hit by a car? You see, we confuse being intelligent, which we are inherently, with fear and paranoia and then think that we're safer because we're afraid and paranoid. But you don't have to be either of these not to step in front of a car. That's just intelligent.

We can trust ourselves if we're in the present moment. Most people who are hit by cars* we can guess, aren't present, aren't paying attention.

*Read "hit by cars" as a metaphor with broad application.

35

(a) Most of us say that we want to be happy and we believe that we do, but we lead ourselves astray with this belief. If we really wanted to be happy, we'd be happy. Happy is what's there when we stop doing everything else. In truth, we prefer almost anything other than happiness. We will leave our happiness for almost anything.

I want to be happy, but...

Notice that anytime we say "but" we negate whatever came first in our sentence. We can doze through the first of someone's sentence of explanation and wake up for the post "but" information:

> I would like to have dinner with
> you, but...
> He's very nice, but...
> I wanted to help, but...

After the but comes the real message. I want to be happy, but I hate my job. I want to be happy, but I'm overweight. I want to be happy, but my mother drives me crazy.

I want to be happy, but...

I prefer to be judgmental; I prefer to beat myself; I prefer to focus on what I don't have, etc.

If you want to be happier

be happier <u>NOW</u>

in <u>THIS</u> moment.

(If you're paying close attention you will probably hear a voice in your head say something like, " But that's irresponsible. That's denying reality." That voice speaks out of fear, not clarity. You <u>are</u> equal to your life. That voice, and others, don't trust this to be true. Gently reassure them.)

We are equal

to our lives.

Sit in compassion

In the
present moment...

and watch what happens.

It is not logical.

We spend an inordinate amount of time maintaining our suffering. You can be insisting that you're not; in fact, you could be screaming at the top of your lungs that you're not. But you are.

The thing that most of us are afraid of more than anything else is that we might even briefly get in touch with our True Nature. You might even be sitting in meditation, all the while fearful that you will awaken.

It is not logical.

We continue, daily, to make comfortable decisions that maintain our suffering — comfortable suffering — no-risk suffering. If we were to awaken, the game would be over.

So don't try to figure out how this works. We are trained to say one thing and do another.

Whoever thought up this game did a good job. And if you can step back from it enough, maybe you can begin to appreciate it for being the way it is.

A basic assumption to which we cling:

I have to __make__ life happen. If
I don't, it won't be the way I
want it to be.

We're so desperately invested in this
assumption that we won't risk allowing
life simply to be the way it is for even
a moment to find out whether or not
we would like it.

And of course this is not an
accident because if we accepted things
the way they are and __liked__ it, what
would our function be? What would we
do all day? Since we spend all day
controlling life, we'd be out of work.

"This practice emphasizes acceptance —
acceptance of everything. That sounds like
a do-nothing approach to life. How can
we bring about change if we accept
everything as it is? What would motivate us to act? What would get us out
of bed in the morning? It all sounds so
passive."

The acceptance we emphasize demands
our full attention, our complete willingness,
our unconditional love, and our deepest
wisdom and compassion. There is nothing
passive about it.

We confuse "giving up" with "acceptance."
They are very different. Giving up is the
experience of ego: there is a sense of
defeat, of being a victim, of being
separate from and oppressed by "them,"
and a strong desire for things to be
different even though we have given up
trying to change them — there is no
acceptance in it, only resignation.

In the world of duality, acceptance, like
everything else, brings with it the possibility of its opposite: rejection. When we
speak of acceptance in these terms we

are describing it from ego's point of view. Ego says, "Sure, I can accept that." This is not unconditional acceptance — we know if what has been accepted changes into something ego doesn't like, the acceptance will quickly vanish. Acceptance of this kind is simply a matter of liking and disliking, an experience that can eventually lead to passivity. We get tired of liking and disliking; we become overwhelmed by so many choices; we become apathetic.

The acceptance we emphasize in this practice has no opposite. It embraces everything, including the world of duality and opposites. And because it brings us fully into the present moment, acceptance of this kind takes us into a realm of no choice. When we are fully present to what is, there is no question of non-acceptance or resistance or rejection — things just are. And because ego isn't present to like or dislike, or to feel separate from what is, we also experience ourselves just as we are, and we sense our oneness with everything. We find that this acceptance includes us, too. We see that we are not the bestowers of acceptance; we are acceptance.

"But still — what about change? What about social injustice and cruelty — how can we bring about change if we aren't making choices, if we just go around accepting everything? How can we change something by being one with it?"

How can we change something in any other way? By being one with the present moment, we experience full acceptance. Nothing escapes us; nothing is denied. We see it all. And we move with it. And in moving with it we are able to respond appropriately to what is happening right now. We have food to share with someone who's hungry? We share it. Saddened by cruelty to animals? We stop eating meat. Interested in helping out in the ghettos? We volunteer. We offer ourselves in love and oneness, out of a sense of us all being in this together.

How arrogant it is for us to think that our rejection of something changes it. Do we eliminate hunger by rejecting it? Or do we accept it as a fact of life for many of us and respond accordingly? Do we alleviate the suffering of abused children with our disapproval? Of course not. We like to believe that we do — it makes us

44

feel better — but our rejection, denial, and disapproval only affect us. What we reject, deny, or disapprove of will be what it is. Our non-acceptance doesn't change anything. Things change because they change; that is their nature. Everything is in a constant state of flux. While we're busy rejecting "what is," "what is" becomes "what was" and leaves us in its wake. We can't change something that has escaped us.

When we attack injustice, cruelty, and suffering with intolerance and loathing, when we whip ourselves into doing good by telling ourselves that we're bad when left to our own devices, we make the mistake of believing that hatred can generate compassion and goodness. Hatred is suffering, and can only perpetuate suffering, not alleviate it.

Change that arises from duality is change in content only — the whats change but the hows remain the same. The oppressed become the oppressors. We only change roles. Profound change — change in how we do, not what we do — happens only with complete acceptance. Acceptance

45

that goes beyond the dualities of right and wrong, them and us, good and bad. Complete acceptance and profound change are inseparable.

"Okay, let's take the example of hunger. If I hear that people are starving in Africa and I say, 'All right, I accept that,' it sounds to me as if I'm saying that I don't care or maybe even that I like it or approve of it, and if that's the case, I won't do anything about it."

Remember that the acceptance we're pointing to here has nothing to do with liking and disliking, caring or not caring. The kind of acceptance we're talking about embraces liking and disliking as it does all dualities but it is not defined by them. Using this example from the perspective of this practice, our acceptance of starvation only means that we accept that people are _in fact_ starving — in other words, we don't deny it. When we don't deny the reality of something, we can respond to it.

"Well, of course, I have to accept the fact that people are starving if I'm going to do something about it. But if I just accept the fact of starvation without hating the suffering that goes with it; what would motivate me to help?"

Your inherent goodness. The compassion that is in your heart when you stop pushing suffering away.

We all have a natural capacity for helping, for responding lovingly and compassionately. When we step back from the voices that are always telling us how things should be and how we should react— when we are not identified with ego — we provide an opportunity to experience this inherent goodness. And from this experience of inherent goodness, and in our acceptance of all that is, we learn to trust our natural inclination to follow the path that leads away from suffering. We learn to respond lovingly and appropriately. We become responsible in the truest sense of the word.

Stay flexible.

Everything
changes
all the time.

It is far better to do something wrong than to live one's life in fear of doing something wrong.

There is no such thing as a mistake. "Mistake" is an idea we use to torture ourselves. When we pay attention, everything enlightens us.

"Everything in life comes to you as a teacher.
Pay attention.
Learn quickly."

— Old Cherokee woman to her grandson

WORRYING
ABOUT DOING
THE WRONG THING

IS NOT THE RIGHT THING TO DO.

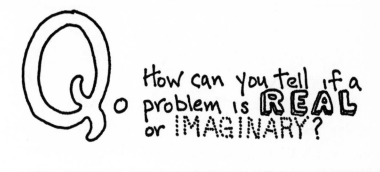

Q. How can you tell if a problem is **REAL** or IMAGINARY?

A. If it doesn't have a solution, it's imaginary.

"It seems that when I plan and work toward something that I _make_ it happen. You say it doesn't work that way. Please explain."

We don't make life happen — we're a manifestation in form of Life. We go in a certain natural direction. We have certain natural tendencies and predispositions, talents and gifts. We have a physical being, mental capabilities, conditioning, and influences that form us and move us in a certain direction. We will go in that direction as everything in life is going in its direction. We're a part of Life.

At some point I decide that I would like to be a pilot (or plumber or journalist). I ask myself, "Do I have the capabilities? Are the circumstances right? In the same sense that everything must come together for a plant to grow and flourish from a seed, are they coming together for this to grow and flourish?"

I move in whatever direction I am drawn.

If I want to be a pilot I study, I take lessons, I learn to fly. I do whatever I need to do to reach my goal. The place where I could get into trouble would be in believing that because I'm going in a certain direction, it means I'm going to wind up in a certain place.

The fact that I want to be a pilot and that I study and train doesn't mean I'll ever become one. And if I don't, it doesn't mean there's anything wrong with me or life or the universe or anything else. It just means that it didn't happen, in the same way that a plant can be growing along and suddenly there's a late freeze and it dies.

And if I do reach my goal it doesn't mean I was able to manipulate the flow of events and achieve a certain outcome through the force of my own will. It just happened, influenced by all that preceeded it since before the beginning of beginningless time.

Sit down in a comfortable position that enables you to keep your back straight. Relax your abdomen, drop your shoulders. Let your eyes rest 3 or 4 feet in front of you. Take a few deep breaths and then let your breathing return to normal.

Feel your body breathing. Feel the air enter your body, fill your body, and leave your body.

Thoughts will arise and pass away. Feelings will arise and pass away. You may hear sounds, smell odors, see sights, feel sensations. Just notice them, resisting nothing, holding onto nothing (resisting no thing, holding onto no thing), allowing everything to be as it is.

Just sit— not trying to accomplish anything, not trying to change anything, especially yourself. Breathe in and breathe out.

Aware   Right here
Alert   Right now
Attentive   Accepting what is
Present   Simply noticing

Want to make a contribution to the whole world?

Okay, end your own suffering.

(What? Ending your own suffering sounds self indulgent?

It isn't.
It's the most responsible thing you could ever do.)

"What does 'letting go' mean? Letting go of what? How is it different from getting rid of something?"

Is it possible to get rid of something? We can repress, reject, and resist until we've blue in the face, and still not be rid of something. By burying, hiding, denying, and then refusing to look, we fool ourselves into believing that we've gotten rid of something when really all we've done is close our eyes. Getting rid of something is ego's way of handling what ego doesn't like or want. It is based on the illusion of separateness and duality, namely that ego ("I") is separate or different from whatever it finds objectionable. Ego assumes that it has control over this unwanted something else, and can get rid of it whenever it wants to.

Letting go allows us to see that we were never in control in the first place. (Ego will not find this information reassuring, so be prepared for the usual backlash: "What do you mean I'm not in control? If I'm not, then who is? If I can't control my life, what will become of me? What about freedom of choice?" And so on.)

"But do you really mean that I have no control over my life?"

Not in the sense that we usually mean it. You can write the script, but you'll need a lot of cooperation for the play to go the way you've written it. That's a lot to expect, especially when you consider that everyone else has a script that doesn't read anything like yours. You can make plans, you can make decisions, you can make choices, but there's no guarantee that things will go the way you expect or want them to. When you can see that, when you can act without attachment to the outcome, you are acting from the center that knows it does not control life, but is life itself.

"How is letting go different from giving up?"

Giving up, like "getting rid of," is the experience of ego, specifically the experience of a defeated separate self. When we give up, we feel as if we have lost control, having relinquished it unwillingly to someone or something more powerful than we are. We see ourselves as victims. We've already said that letting go allows us to see that life doesn't control us. It allows us to see that we are life.

Letting go is releasing our grip on delusion, allowing us to see what is. When we stop resisting what is, when we stop clinging to our beliefs and assumptions about how things should be, we are letting go, we are opening ourselves to the present moment.

Letting go goes hand in hand with acceptance. One does not occur without the other. Letting go is opening the hand. Acceptance is what the open hand receives.

"To get along in the world don't we often have to just push our fears aside and make decisions about things?"

The first thing to consider here is that there is nothing more important than compassion. Nothing. There is nothing that needs to be done, nothing that needs to be improved, not if the price we must pay is to lose compassion. In terms of this question, it's good to explore "who" is deciding that "pushing aside" the frightened parts of ourselves is the thing to do.

Let's look at an example. A part of me, let's call her Rose, decides that my life has gone stale and that what I need to do is move, change residences. Another part of me, Mary, is afraid and insecure and doesn't want to move. She approaches major changes cautiously and would usually prefer to maintain the status quo.

Mary begins to undermine Rose's resolve so Rose's attitude becomes something like, "I've got to just whip Mary into shape. She's a weak, scared person, and if I listen to her, I'll never be able to get on with my life and do the things I need to do."

If I see moving / not moving as the only issue in this situation, I haven't looked deeply enough. The important thing here is the relationship between Rose and Mary. Unless I look at that carefully, find out about it, and let it go, I'll make the same contest out of every aspect of my life. Today it's moving, tomorrow it's job, relationship, health, finances. I'll have a lifetime of having a part of me beat up and push away another part of me for being frightened. Punishment does not alleviate fear.

If I seek clarity and freedom from fear, the only route is compassion for all the players in my internal drama. Because when I look deeply enough, it becomes clear that Rose is as frightened of stagnation as Mary is of change.

There is nothing more important than compassion.

The two sides of the
coin of control.

We hide things from ourselves when we're afraid to see what's there. When we're willing to accept ourselves just as we are, we have nothing to fear.

"If you want to end your suffering, stop identifying with the process that's causing it."

We stop identifying with the process that maintains our suffering when we stop judging ourselves, when we stop holding a club over our heads to make sure we do things right.

The moment we drop all of that, we have dropped the only thing that can cause us to suffer.

Choose a day and, from the time you wake up until the time you go to sleep, keep as accurate a list as you can of each time you _in_ _any_ _way_ criticise, abandon, beat, or otherwise disapprove of yourself.

Watch closely. We abandon ourselves on some deep levels that seem so "normal" we tend to overlook them.

When we are faced with performing a difficult task, we think our choices are:

1) Feel pressure, stress, fear, and panic and do it right.

2) Do it wrong.

Many people feel that we need to be stressful in order to be efficient and effective. It's the old, "I work better under pressure."

Nobody works better under pressure. Nobody. It might take a lot of pressure to make someone work, but that doesn't mean they've working better.

Assumption:
If you're not hysterical, it means that you've not paying attention, that you don't really understand the problem.

"I'm a perfectionist."
"I'm a people-pleaser."
"I'm an approval seeker."

These are examples of ways we have of describing ourselves that help us explain our approach to life and why life is so often hard for us. Perhaps we could look closer.

Being a perfectionist is not a problem— I want everything done as well as it can be done in this moment. The problem is that I'm really an imper- fectionist. I'm not actually looking for that which is perfect, I'm seek- ing the imperfect. I will examine and change standards until the goal is impossible then I will label that goal "perfection". The next step is to beat myself for failing to meet my perfec- tionist ideals.

But, in fact, I have met my ideal, my true goal. I believe myself to be imperfect and I have proven it.

In the same vein, I am a people- displeaser. No matter how many times

I have pleased others, I won't start counting until someone is not pleased. Then my response is, "See, I can never do it right." But I have. I am looking to displease someone and I've just done it. I'm right! That's what I thought I'd do. I have been true to my <u>real</u> belief.

There is the belief we believe we believe
and then there is
what we really believe.

Perhaps we could look deeper into our beliefs about seeking approval and helping others and being good.

If I say I want to be good and
only count the times I'm not,
what am I really trying to prove?

We always choose our beliefs over our experience.

The only way I can maintain
my beliefs
is by never examining them.

I just have to adopt them, believe them,
and never scrutinize them. And the best
way of all is never to say them out
loud. Just operate off belief systems
that I never say to another human being,
then nobody's going to challenge me. I'll
never have to listen to anyone else's
ideas. I can stay in my safe, familiar
little world.

It's difficult to own our freedom.

We are so privileged that we have to ignore vast areas of our lives in order to pick out just those things that aren't the way we want them to be. This process of ignoring and selective perception lets us continue to see ourselves as victims of life circumstances.

We're addicted to being victims.

And it is only by remaining victims ourselves that we can continue to justify victimizing others.

In order to remain a victim,
you can't know how to be master.

But if there were no brass ring, it
would be no fun to be on the merry-
go-round.

So the idea is to know how
to grab the ring and then MISS!
right at the last second.

Benefits:

You don't have to take responsibility.
You get to stay on the merry-go-round.
You get to remain a victim.

"What are 'subpersonalities'?"

We use this term to refer to aspects of ourselves, the different ways we can be and behave: for instance, one minute I might feel completely irresistible and wonderfully competent, and the next, unloved and worth-less. Subpersonalities act as though they have lives of their own, but their survival and identity actually depend upon other subpersonalities — both within ourselves and others.

When we say we want one thing and always seem to end up with another, we can suspect a subpersonality at work. Let's say I'm aware of wanting to be loved, but the people I'm involved with treat me indifferently, and the more I try to get them to love me, the less responsive they become until finally they tell me to get lost. This happens over and over again. I never have the love I say I want. Why not?

When I look for an answer in terms of a subpersonality, I begin to see an interesting pattern. I'll call the part of myself who wants to be loved Jane. Jane is small, shy, and socially ill at ease. She craves love, but really doesn't see herself as lovable. As with any subpersonality, Jane's survival and identity are always at stake. If she actually feels loved, what will happen to that identity? What will become of her?

Jane doesn't want to find out. Jane wants to be Jane even though it means going through hell. She begins by stating her case with two opposing beliefs: "I want to be loved/I'm unlovable." Both beliefs are indispensable in maintaining her identity — the belief that she wants to be loved sets the scene for proving that she's unlovable. She's on her way.

If I picture Jane as an abstract drawing, I see her as a circle with certain receptors on her circumference. She looks around until she finds someone, another circle, with complementary receptors; they lock into each other. It's important to know that Jane's perception of "complementary receptors" is just that: her perception or projection. Whether the other person actually has these complementary receptors is beside the point. Jane will perceive the relationship the way she wants it to be.

Before too long Jane starts to feel ignored, or unloved, or not loved enough. Once again her "unlovability" is confirmed. Although miserable, she has what she wants. She would rather be right than happy.

We create subpersonalities in response to our experience and conditioning. They are coping mechanisms — predictable, familiar, safe ways of dealing with what life brings us. One subpersonality begets another until the stage is so crowded and the dialogues so numerous that trying to untangle them all to see who's who can seem overwhelming. But if we can start with just one and isolate it long enough for close examination, we begin to see more clearly, too, and from there we begin to see how interrelated they all are, and how they support and feed off one another.

Here's how it works in Jane's case. Being unloved is hard and painful. It's not surprising, then, that Jane is often seen in the company of Rambo, her "protector" subpersonality. Rambo gets even with the creeps who've treated her badly. But Rambo is dangerous. We need someone more civilized to do his job so we don't all get arrested. So along comes By the Book who will do the job legally, and then, in the name of fairness, we have the judge, and then the jury, and the media... It goes on and on.

We find the model of subpersonalities useful as a means of stepping back from the melodrama of our lives. When we can do this and are not so caught up in the identity of a particular subpersonality, we can look again to see where we are. Have we stepped into another subpersonality? Maybe. If so, we can keep stepping back until there's no where else to step because we're right here— at the center of our true nature.

There is what is

and to that we add shoulds and
oughts and musts and pressures and
guilts and fears and paranoias and
anxieties and attitudes and beliefs

and to make it worse
we add these things after the fact!

We complicate things endlessly.

Our job is to see clearly how we get
ourselves tangled up and then be
willing to disentangle ourselves —
which we are once we've really seen
what we're doing and how we're
doing it.

Our biggest obstacle

is that we have so many attitudes
about how we <u>should</u> be, we keep
ourselves incapable of seeing what is.

Remaining ignorant is a full-time job.

The truth is always here...

We have to work hard not to see it.

"What is projection?"

It is seeing the world through our experience.

I can only know me — my thoughts and my feelings. I can't know yours in the same way. You can describe them to me, but still, without getting inside your skin I am not going to know you in the same way I can know myself. So if I look at you and say to myself, " He is very happy today, very friendly," I am basing that on my experience of being happy and friendly — either my experience of being happy and friendly right now or in the past. If I'm feeling happy and friendly right now, then I am projecting those feelings onto you. I am happy and friendly so I see you as happy and friendly.

But let's say I don't feel happy and friendly at all, but instead, tired and grumpy, and I still see you as happy and friendly. I am basing that on my past experience of happy and friendly. In other words I interpret what you're doing and saying as happy and friendly because

In the past, when I have behaved as I see you are behaving now, I was happy and friendly.

Projection doesn't mean that I'm never going to know anything about you since I can only know myself. You may or may not be happy and friendly today. If you are, then my projection is "correct" in that my experience of happiness and friendliness coincides with yours. If you're not, then I am mistaken. But the point is not whether I am "right" or "wrong" about you. It doesn't matter. What matters is knowing that when I perceive someone else as happy and friendly, or sneaky and dishonest, or loyal and loving, I am perceiving myself. I cannot know what I have not experienced. I cannot perceive goodness in you without having known it in myself.

"If projection is an experience of myself put on others — my interpretation of the world based only on my experience— it seems like something I should stop. It seems wrong somehow — as if I might be missing some bigger truth that I am unable to see because I can only know my experience."

There is nothing wrong with projection. It comes to us naturally. It is what we do— it is not something we can stop or should even want to stop.

The danger lies in not recognizing projection for what it is, in not being aware of it. If I say that my neighbor is a barbarian and don't understand that I can't know that about him without having experienced the barbarian in myself, then I separate myself from him. I think I'm better than he is. Pretty soon, I might even think he needs to be punished. I see "barbaric" as something "out there," not in here. There is conflict; maybe even war. There is suffering.

If, on the other hand, I admire another neighbor as the most wonderful, kindest person I ever met and don't understand that I can't know that about her without having experienced myself as wonderful and kind, then I separate myself from her, too. I think she's better than I am. I might want her to be my friend, hoping that by association she will make me wonderful and kind. I see "wonderful and kind" as something "out there," not in here. I feel deficient, inadequate. I am suffering.

By projecting we are not necessarily missing a bigger truth. We miss that truth through our lack of awareness. When we look outside of ourselves for answers, when we blame a neighbor, when we seek our happiness in externals, we are turning our backs on this bigger truth, the truth of ourselves. When projection has awareness, it brings us back to ourselves, back to this truth. We see our contradictions, our strengths, our weaknesses — we see that we are everything we thought was "out there." And when we are able to see that, when we are able to see that we are everything, it is because we are looking from the center of our being. We are looking from our True Nature, the biggest truth of all.

I'm constantly comparing
the way I think life should be
to the way life is.

I have broken everything down
into
good and bad.

Everything that is the way I want it to be
is good.
Things that aren't the way I want them
to be are bad.

GOOD	BAD
GOOD HEALTH: the way I want to feel	BAD GOVERNMENT: holds policies I don't agree with
GOOD SPOUSE: needs as much attention as I want to give	BAD PERSON: does things I would never do
GOOD PHILOSOPHY OF LIFE: validates who I am and what I believe in	BAD RULE: one I don't want to follow
etc.	etc.

We form a subject/object relationship with everything that comes into
our awareness. We constantly compare
things and form judgments. "I like
this; I don't like that. This is a waste
of time; that is worthwhile. This is
Truth; that is delusion." You get
the idea.

It's a full-time job keeping
everything in its place and also
endlessly entertaining comparing the
same things over and over again
just to make sure we got it right
the first time.

This doesn't accomplish anything.
It just makes us feel secure.

When we're living in the present moment, life is very easy. It's not that living in the present means only good and pleasant things happen to us. It is an attitude of mind as well as an actual experience of seeing that whatever happens is perfect.

In the present we see that life is happening exactly as it "should"— exactly as it is. When we realize that we are a part of that perfection and realize it's not possible for us to be separate from it, except through our own delusion of separation (ego), then we experience our lives as easy.

When we separate ourselves out, when we identify with a small, egocentric, separate self, then life becomes hard. Because that's when we're trying to make life happen.

I get an idea about how life should be, about how I should be, and then I set out to make that happen. A great deal of the time my idea about what should be is just NOT what's going on in the universe. And so I'm constantly in conflict. People are not behaving the way I want them to; my car breaks down; I'm late for an appointment. I'm constantly comparing the way I think life should be to the way life is.

As soon as we let go of the notion that there is the possibility of a life other than the one that is, we move away from suffering and into a deeper level of peace and acceptance.

Remember,
you don't have to go anywhere, you don't
have to get anything. Nothing needs to
change. You are exactly where you
need to be; you're doing exactly what
you need to do. (You can know this
is true because this is where you
are, and this is what you've doing.)
When you know this, everything becomes
your teacher.

You can't get away from your opportunity to see how you are. You can
ignore it, but you can't get away
from it. If you try, then it just becomes your opportunity to see how you
do ignore-ance.

There isn't some other reality that
would be a better chance for you to
see yourself than this one.
This is it.
Pay attention.

Sit still.
Listen.

Can you hear your thoughts?

What are they saying?

Anything new?

"How can I tell the difference between what ego is telling me to do and what my heart is telling me to do?"

Egocentricity is having a better idea about how this moment should be. Egocentricity is the process of, the result of, being able to experience ourselves as separate from the present. It is being able to perceive ourselves as being other than our own heart. Ego talks in terms of "This is right... This is wrong... I have to do this... A person must..."—phrases like that. When we are listening to egocentricity we have the feeling that we know beyond doubt how we should be operating and how life should be.

Our heart doesn't tell us what to do. Being at one with our heart means simply being present to and appropriate in the current circumstances. Following the voice of our heart, the message is very subtle. It's so subtle that we have been trained or have trained ourselves not to hear it. The voice of our heart doesn't talk in terms of shoulds. Instead, we sense a direction. We have a feeling, a notion, on a subtle level that this is so or that is so.

If somebody were to say, "How do you know you're doing the right thing?" the response would probably be something like, "I can't be sure that I'm right. It just feels like my heart is guiding me to do this."

We are so concerned about being

It might be helpful to consider:

- As long as you want to be right you'll be wrong.

- When you accept that you're wrong you'll be right.

- The only way to be right is to be wrong.

SMALL MIND:

operates in the world of duality -
sees things in black and white and
shades of gray - holds beliefs -
holds grudges - falls in love - cops
an attitude - wants to be under-
stood - knows its boundaries -
resists unwanted change - makes
judgements - fears death - fears
life - delights in luxury - condemns
excess - abhors civilization -
destroys rain forests - assumes
superiority - assumes inferiority -
ad infinitum

WHOLE MIND:

-ad infinitum

What would happen if I

    let go of all my defenses
    lived in the present
    let myself off the hook
    put all my energy into enjoying
       my life
    stopped believing the things I
       tell myself
    loved myself unconditionally ?

Would I

    quit my job
    wind up on the street
    go hungry
    become greedy and selfish
    let others run over me
    lose my self respect
    turn into a criminal
    be bored ?

       Risk it.

We lose everything. Husbands, wives, lovers, families, friends, possessions, our egos, our bodies — everything. Sooner or later. One way or another. Quickly or over a long period of time. We keep nothing of this world.

Usually, though, we manage to overlook or to deny that we lose everything, that we die. We might accept this as a fact of life for other people when we allow ourselves to think about it, but we're careful to keep it at a safe distance. "They" suffer; "they" die. "We" don't.

But as long as we keep this knowledge at arms length where we see loss as something that happens to others, then we are not really seeing it at all. And any act to alleviate the suffering of others will spring from this sense of separateness — quite possibly out of a feeling of superiority, or moral obligation, rather than from true compassion. This "kindness" might do more harm than good.

But when we drop our defenses and permit ourselves to experience the absolute reality of loss, not just as someone else's, but as _our_ loss, it is very hard not to feel compassion for ourselves and for others. How can we be unkind to someone who not only loses everything s/he has, but will never even have most of what s/he wants?

The important word here is "compassion." It is very different from feeling sorry for ourselves or for someone else. "Feeling sorry for" is something our separate selves experience. It is the experience of someone who thinks suffering is something that happens to other people.

When we truly experience loss and suffering and compassion, we sometimes feel that our hearts are breaking. We feel so much pain that often our first impulse is to rebuild our defenses. But if we can stay with that pain without resorting to anger and denial, then we have the chance to experience who we really are, to be reunited with our intrinsic purity, that energy or force that is all love, all joy, and all goodness. We lose everything, but in experiencing the essence of that loss, we are reunited with all that is.

It is inaccurate to equate

> pain and suffering
> loss and suffering
> hunger and suffering
> sickness and suffering
> poverty and suffering

It is also inaccurate to equate

> wealth and happiness
> good fortune and happiness
> abundance and happiness
> health and happiness
> beauty and happiness

Whether life is seen as a struggle
or a gift depends on one's attitude
of mind, not on one's circumstances.

We are conditioned to believe that if I'm on my side, I'm against yours. We're conditioned to an attitude of mind of deprivation, a belief in "not enough", and so we're constantly struggling for "our share," believing that we're lacking, trying to get more. We wind up always seeking better accommodation, assuming that we're going to lose out if we've not ever vigilant.

The place we're moving toward in spiritual practice is one of plenty. When I realize I have all I need in each moment, more than enough, I can begin to be generous. So "taking my own side" is not a matter of quantity or even quality in the sense of getting my share; it's a matter of compassion. It is simply realizing how hard it is to be a human being, how cruel and unloving has been our conditioning and then not wanting to add to anyone's suffering — not even our own.

Taking my own side can only happen when I am willing to let go of my ideas of deprivation and loss and inadequacy and move into that place that has no sides, no separation, no "other", that place that includes, that is all. Then it's not a question of my side or your side; it's our side.

We need to have $o mu¢h
money be¢au$e we're trying
to ¢ompen$ate our$elve$

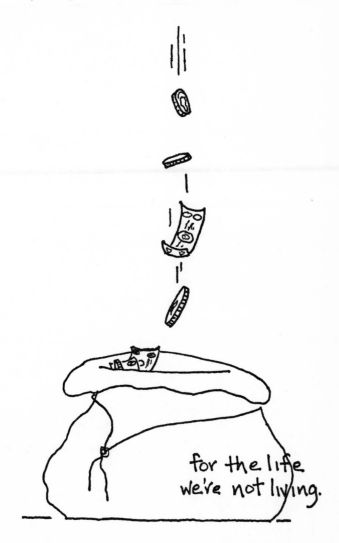

for the life
we're not living.

The only thing that threatens you

LIFE
SICKNESS
REJECTION
PAIN
DEATH
LONELINESS

is that of which
you are ignorant.

I identify with a role, a certain way of being, without realizing that by doing so I have sharply limited myself.

From this role, I look around at the world and judge, categorize, accept, and reject everything I see:
   "I'm not like that."
   "I support that view."
   "I can't/won't do that."
   "I like this way."

I close the door on anything that doesn't support my chosen identity. Out of a vast wealth of possibilities, I choose one narrow little section and call that "me."

The moment I find the courage to open even one of those closed doors, I have chosen to follow my heart.

"What about anger? All my life I've been taught that I shouldn't get angry. I learned the lesson so well that for a long time I thought I never was angry—about anything—and now I'm beginning to see that that isn't true. I've just been repressing it. And now sometimes I feel mad enough to kill. I don't know what to do with this anger and wonder what it means."

One of the precepts of our practice is "Not to be angry." Not "Not to get angry," but "Not to be angry." At first not being angry might sound more impossible than not getting angry, but it's not. If we feel anger, and are telling ourselves not to show it, then we will repress it. This is very hard to do. We tense up. We get stomach aches and headaches, not to mention depressed and sullen. All because we think we shouldn't be angry.

There are no "shoulds" in this practice. If we're angry, we're angry, and it's good for us to know that we are angry, and to not deny it. What is, is. But what can we do with this anger so that we're not adding to the world's suffering by taking it out on others? What do we do with all that energy? We can take a long, hard walk. We can pound nails. We can punch a pillow. And we can talk about it. This all comes under the heading of "getting angry." There is nothing wrong with it. It can lead us to other discoveries.

When we can acknowledge our anger, we can begin to acknowledge other feelings as well, feelings that are often buried under the anger. Eventually we might realize that when we're angry, we've also hurt or frightened or sad, and that we are trying to avoid the pain of those emotions by being angry. We begin to suspect that anger misses the point, that anger is a secondary emotion. We see that it arises out of our pain because anger makes us feel powerful. We feel protected when we're angry. We feel right or even righteous.

The precept "Not to be angry" is pointing us toward seeing anger as a defense. It reminds us to look for the pain beneath the anger. It asks, "What are we protecting ourselves against?"

There is no precept that says "Don't feel pain." Not being angry allows us to see the source of our pain. When we can see that, we can also see our way through it.

We are equal to our present moment experience...

...we can always put the next foot down.

"What brings us to a meditation practice? Is it ego seeking 'better accommodation' through enlightenment? Or is it something else?"

Sometimes ego brings us to a practice like this. Perhaps our lives haven't been going well, and ego is willing to consider a meditation practice as a means of regaining control. Or maybe we've been shopping around for new experiences, new highs — a kind of spiritual materialism that makes us feel exciting and important. If these kinds of reasons bring us to a practice like this, and if, once in the practice, there is no new awareness of how we are motivated, then as soon as we feel better (in the case of life not going well) or things start to get boring (in the case of looking for excitement) we'll move on to something else, leaving this practice behind with the rationalization that we have either outgrown it or it's just not working for us anymore.

We suspect, though, that more often than not, the reason we are drawn to a practice like this is because ego, worn down from having suffered long and hard, quietly acquiesces to the wisdom of the heart. We are looking for something beyond our suffering from the only place that is beyond suffering: our true nature, our essential being, our oneness, our wholeness. The one doing the seeking is the one being sought. Of course, once on the spiritual path, ego can quickly reassert itself, finding all kinds of reasons for not continuing — most of which arise out of its extreme discomfort at being scrutinized. When this happens, it helps to remember the intuitive wisdom that first prompted us to look inward.

"How do we get so far away from our true nature? How 'true' can it be if it's so easy to lose sight of?"

Abandoning ourselves (our true nature) is a conditioning process that begins the moment we're born. The beliefs and assumptions of parents, siblings, teachers, friends, and the society as a whole become so ingrained in us that our identities soon become tied to either rejecting those beliefs or making them our own. We start seeing ourselves in terms of "I'm the kind of person who..." or "That's just the way I am." We identify ourselves by what we like and dislike, by what we believe and don't believe. Because the conditioning is so loud, so aggressive, so relentless, and so pervasive, it soon blinds us to the still, quiet presence of our true nature, and deafens us to the "voice" of our hearts.

When we abandon ourselves, we leave that center of peace and plenty, of clarity and wisdom, of love and compassion for the source of our suffering — that illusion of separateness that is conflict and deprivation, confusion and ignorance, hatred and rejection.

When we look to externals to make us happy, when we are preoccupied with arranging the "whats" of our lives so that we can avoid pain, we have abandoned ourselves. We have abandoned our intrinsic purity and adequacy in favor of a belief in our defectiveness.

This practice points us toward the true

nature we abandoned long ago. Some of us still have a sense of that presence; some of us don't. It is available to all of us. We may have left it but it hasn't left us. It's still here. When we have enough interest in ending our suffering, when we drop our defenses and look, we open the door to reuniting ourselves with this presence, our essential being.

It takes a tremendous
act of courage♡

to admit

to yourself

that you are not

DEFECTIVE

in any way

whatsoever.

 Sit down in a comfortable position that enables you to keep your back straight. Relax your abdomen, drop your shoulders. Let your eyes rest 3 or 4 feet in front of you. Take a few deep breaths and then let your breathing return to normal.

Feel your body breathing. Feel the air enter your body, fill your body, and leave your body.

Thoughts will arise and pass away. Feelings will arise and pass away. You may hear sounds, smell odors, see sights, feel sensations. Just notice them, resisting nothing, holding onto nothing (resisting no thing, holding onto no thing), allowing everything to be as it is.

Just sit— not trying to accomplish anything, not trying to change anything, especially yourself. Breathe in and breathe out.

Aware   Right here
Alert   Right now
Attentive   Accepting what is
Present   Simply noticing

We define who we are
by what we
accept
and
reject.

PERSON #1

ACCEPTS	REJECTS
conservative politics	beans and rice
expensive vacations	eastern religion
croissants and gelato	liberal politics
designer jeans	overalls

PERSON #2

ACCEPTS	REJECTS
tofu burgers	quiche
yoga	aerobics classes
Mother Jones	Business Week
organic gardening	golf

Your definition of who you are is your
prison. You can set yourself free at
any time.

"So, how can I see through all this?"

Pay attention.

"And...?"

That's all, just pay attention. You don't have to do anything, change anything, fix anything, know anything, understand anything — just pay attention.

It's like this: Suppose you go to bed one night in your own home. All the doors and windows are locked, you're in the house alone. The next morning when you go to make coffee, the coffee pot is gone. You look for it, ransack your memory trying to recall what you did with it. Then you have to go to work. (Really imagine that this is happening to you and picture what you'd do.)

The next morning you get up with an alternate plan for coffee, since you never did find the pot, walk into the kitchen and the stove is gone. What do you do? Question your sanity? Become frightened? Do you think about who could have a key to the house, look for what else is missing, call your friends, call the police?

The next morning you get up and enter the kitchen cautiously. Everything seems okay. Whew! You reach over to turn on the news and, oops! the TV is gone!

What are you going to do? Hire a detective? Change all the locks? Move? Perhaps you might consider not going to sleep. Perhaps you might decide to stay up, stay wide awake and <u>watch</u> until you can see <u>how</u> this is happening.

There's an old Zen story about a fellow who is going off to war and is in such a hurry that he neglects to see to his spiritual well-being before he goes. The closer he gets to battle the more anxious he becomes about his unanswered questions. Finally he's in such a state that one of the other soldiers tells him of a Zen master living nearby and suggests that the fellow go visit. He rides over, asks for an interview and when it's granted, asks the teacher if he knows the secret to life.

The teacher nods.

"Will you tell me?" pleads the soldier. "I am off to war and can not know if I will survive."

The master says simply, "Pay attention."

There is no freedom in good fortune.
(It never comes with a guarantee.)

How wonderful
not to be dependent on it!

One Less Act of Violence

In the hills between Mountain View, where we have a Zen Center, and the Pacific is a protected open space area. It is an exquisitely beautiful place where people can walk, run, bike, and ride horses along miles of roads and trails. The city of Mountain View operates a "working farm" there with pigs, sheep, goats, rabbits, chickens, ducks, and a large garden. The purpose of the farm is to make available to urban families and especially children an experience of a rural lifestyle. There *seems* to be an emphasis on the care and comfort of the animals since people are admonished not to feed or touch them.

One morning I was running in the park, and when I came over the hill above the farm I heard a sound I had never heard before. I could tell it was a creature sound, but something about it was very wrong. The creatures were screaming hysterically. I sped up and quickly came to the entrance of the farm. A sign on the gate said not to enter, that the farm was closed. My heart was pounding. Of course, I had been running, and I was about to go through a gate I had been instructed not to go through, but the pounding of my heart was in response to that horrible sound. A woman came toward me as I went through the gate, holding out her arms as if to bar the way. I walked past her and around the corner of the barn. There, hanging upside down from the back of a butcher's truck, were two of the sheep I had spoken to almost every day of their lives as I ran past. Their legs were tied together, their throats slit. Two men leaned against the truck laughing and chatting. A few feet away, behind the closed barn doors, were the other sheep and goats, screaming in what I can only guess was terror and pain.

Because we are insensitive to animals, we assume that they are insensitive, too. Because they mean nothing to us, it does not occur to us that they have a life experience. We simply do not care. We do not allow ourselves to care. People who do care are considered eccentric, out there on the fringe. After all, they are just animals, not human beings. But what they are is not the point; the point is what we must do to our hearts in order to pretend that they do not matter.

The farm was closed because they did not want the children to know. Unlike most days there were no docents showing groups of wide-eyed little ones what was going on behind the barn. This aspect of "working farm" was kept well hidden from the public. After all, have you ever had to explain to a child that the lamb in lamb chop is the same as the lamb in the field or the storybook? The same lamb Mary had? Have you ever tried to help a child grasp that eating a hamburger requires killing a cow? Their usual reaction is revulsion and disbelief. They often push the hamburger away and refuse to eat it.

But slowly we convince them that you can both love animals and kill them. Yes, we teach them that it is wrong to kill some animals—pets, endangered species—but it is okay to kill others. You can kill for pleasure, that is called "hunting" not "killing," and you can kill for food. It is confusing information for a child to deal with, and yet it is excellent preparation for our approach to killing people: It is wrong to kill people unless they have killed someone or unless we are at war with them or...

Anyone who has ever known and truly loved an animal knows that they are not different from us in any way that would justify their being tortured and murdered. Of course, we very much want them to be different because we want the leather shoes and the sheepskin seat covers and the fried chicken and fish that we pretend is good for us. Some people really, really want to wear the fur and skin of dead animals. We want these things so desperately that we are willing to pretend that we are not doing what we are doing, that creatures are not being murdered, that they do not feel, cry, or scream in terror. We pretend the package on the "meat" counter was not a few days earlier a living, breathing being like ourselves.

2

The irony is that the proof that we know exactly what we are doing is right before us in how we *hide* what we are doing. We use words like "meat," "pork," "steak," "veal," and "leather" instead of "animal flesh," "pig," "cow," "calf," and "cow skin." Slaughterhouses are hidden away. We do not want our children to know where meat comes from until they are old enough to "understand" and to "accept" it. Many children, once they know what it is, attempt to refuse to eat flesh. Most parents force them because it is "good for them," in spite of increasing evidence to the contrary. And the final proof is that most of us will freely admit that if we had to kill the animal and prepare the flesh, liver, heart, or tongue, we would not be "meat" eaters.

I am not writing this to make anyone feel guilty. I ask only that these topics be honestly considered. My real point is not our cruelty toward creatures but what that cruelty and insensitivity does to our own hearts.

If we judge ourselves, if we reject ourselves for who we are and what we do, we are committing an act of violence against ourselves. This is an act of violence we can avoid. If we would simply look closely and consider the ways we are violent, we would stop. Our own acts of violence are ones we have the power to end. But, there are no "shoulds" in this. I do what I do for me, not for "them." The idea is not to change behavior because I judge it to be wrong; the idea is to pay attention. To do something different because I "should" is to miss the point. To be present is the point. When I am present, with my eyes and heart wide open, what do I want to do? Do I really want to eat the flesh of another creature? Of course I like to eat "meat." I grew up eating it. I was conditioned not to think about what it was, who it was, that it lived, drew breath, slept, ate, had babies, was afraid, sought to live. I can't think about that. It's dinner. So of course I like it, of course I want it, of course I would miss it if I were to stop eating it. That's why it is not helpful to stop as a should.

Perhaps a more helpful approach would be to go right on eating as I always have and pay very close attention. Perhaps if I didn't stop the thoughts about this meat, if I were really present to the texture of it, the smell of it, the feel of it under my knife and fork and in my mouth, I would soon choose not to eat it. *Because the real point is not what I am doing to it, the point is what I am doing to me.*

A few years ago I visited the Friends' Meetinghouse in Philadelphia. There I heard this story: William Penn became a Quaker as a grown man. In those days the fashion was for gentlemen to wear a sword. Soon after becoming a Quaker, Penn began to feel uncomfortable about being a member of a nonviolent religion and at the same time wearing a sword, an instrument of violence. He went to a friend who had assisted in his conversion. "What shall I do about this sword?" he asked. The answer was, "Wear it for as long as you can."

Yes, we continue with eyes and heart wide open to what we are doing. We do this not to gather evidence against ourselves so that we have one more reason to beat ourselves up—that just breeds more violence—we watch with open eyes and heart so that we can see clearly and then choose. And if we choose from our heart, the choice will always be compassion for ourselves and all living things. It is really very simple. If the decision, the conclusion, the action is not compassionate, it is not from the heart. We seek the place that is most compassionate for all. If oneself is not included, it is not the place we are seeking. So continue to eat meat, buy leather, go hunting, wear fur, until you no longer want to because to do so hurts your heart. When it hurts more to have the "product" than to do without it, you'll choose not to have it. And it will be a clean choice, a truly harmless, nonviolent choice.

We can approach the subject of violence not as something to feel bad about, not as something to make us feel more deprived and inadequate, not as something to cause us to turn away from our hearts once again and to abandon ourselves further, but rather as a way to return to ourselves, open our hearts, bring joy, peace, comfort, and compassion to life, and to make us feel good about ourselves and one another. Because what we are seeking is the compassion that is who we truly are. We have been turning away from our hearts for so long that we have forgotten that the compassion we seek in within us. It is almost impossible for us to accept this notion as true when it is presented to us. "Oh, but you must mean that I have to *become* a person who can experience compassion. I have to work on myself, improve, be different, and then I'll be able to have compassion for myself." Well, yes and no. It is not true that we need to do anything first, and yet it is true that we will not let ourselves feel that compassion until we feel we deserve it. The best argument for "being good" is that we will allow ourselves to feel good. If we feel we are doing the best we can, we feel we deserve kindness. Now, it is also true that for most of us self-hatred is so deeply entrenched there is almost no chance that we will see ourselves with compassion no matter what we do, and yet even the most ardent self-hater has to be shaken by irrefutable evidence of goodness.

Compassion for the self has nothing to do with self-indulgence. Please don't waste your time with the but-if-I'm-not-hard-on-myself-I'll-just-become-self-indulgent routine. That routine is self-indulgent. Paying attention, catching on to your own "stuff," taking responsibility for it, and cleaning it up is the most unselfish thing we can do for everyone—human and beast.

We cannot be compassionate toward others if we are not compassionate toward ourselves. It is essential that we not approach letting go of our violence as one more should. To do so would make letting go of violence a process of attempting to get rid of violence, and that would be another act of violence against ourselves. The heart is always the highest authority. We can trust the wisdom of the heart, but we must be willing to hear its guidance. The guidance of the heart will always be toward compassion for all.

Often we look out at the condition of the world with a sense of hopelessness. There is so much to be done, so much that is "wrong," what can one person do? Well, one person can do a great deal. We can be kind to ourselves. We can be kind to one another. At every opportunity one person can make a decision toward loving kindness and away from violence. Two pairs of running shoes—one has leather, the other doesn't. Can you choose the non-leather shoes? *This meal* could you not have meat? Not every meal—this meal. Could you use the product not tested on animals? Could you brake for a squirrel? Could you let that person into the traffic ahead of you? Hundreds of opportunities every day. Could you open your heart to a few? Not all, perhaps, but a few? And could you let yourself feel good about your effort? If so, you have already benefited the entire universe. All that is necessary is one small step at a time. In each moment we can choose one less act of violence.

When we turn back to our hearts, when we open to the compassion and are willing to be present to what is, we see the pain very clearly, and the suffering begins to fall away. Suffering is the result of resisting pain, of resisting what is. When we allow pain to simply be, we find that we can embrace it in a compassion that embraces all.

Life is very painful. We share that pain. We have pain in common with all beings. It is a bond we share in living. Our opportunity is to ease the suffering that so often accompanies the pain. I hurt, I know you hurt. I don't want to hurt. It's a small step to I don't want you to hurt. The Golden Rule.

We can take care of each another—all species. All that walks on two, four, six, eight legs; all that crawls, flies, skitters, swims. All us living creatures. Growing up, having young, getting old, getting

6

sick, dying. How much we share! How much we have in common! How much we are alike!

Quotes:

As long as man continues to be the ruthless destroyer of lower living beings, he will never know health or peace. For as long as men massacre animals, they will kill each other. Indeed, he who sows the seed of murder and pain cannot reap joy and love. *Pythagoras*

The greatness of a nation and its moral progress can be judged by the way its animals are treated. *Gandhi*

Until we stop harming all living beings, we are still savages. *Thomas Edison*

My life is full of meaning to me. The life around me must be full of significance to itself. If I am to expect others to respect my life, then I must respect the other life I see. Ethics in our Western world has hitherto been largely limited to the relations of man to man. But that is a limited ethics. We need a boundless ethics that will include the animals also.
Dr. Albert Schweitzer

There can be no double standard. We cannot have peace among men whose hearts find delight in killing any living creature. *Rachel Carson*

Some Statistics:

One lifelong vegetarian saves the lives of more than 1000 animals.

Livestock production consumes more than half of all water used for all purposes in the U.S.

It takes 55 square feet of Latin American land to produce enough grazing area for a single meat patty.

Hundreds of millions of tons of the world's grain harvest are fed to animals. Less than 5 million tons of grain could feed the all the children who starve to death each year.

Over half a million newborn male chicks are thrown away every day because they are not useful for food.

The same amount of land can feed one meat-eater or 20 vegetarians.

No one wants to be hungry. No one wants to be cold. No one wants their baby killed. No one wants to be in pain. No one wants to die, and certainly no one wants to be murdered. I don't. You don't. And no other creature does.

If we could only ask each time we do something that affects the life of another, "How would I feel if this were happening to me?"

As long as we see "them" as the problem and "them" as the power, we are helpless. When I see that I am the problem, I am immediately empowered. It is crucial that we not add the harmful step of self-blame. "If I'm the problem, that means I'm an awful person and it's my fault." But we're not finding fault here, we're finding a solution. If we take the awareness of our own responsibility and turn that into nonviolent action, we begin to move in a direction that ends suffering. I begin to end my suffering when I start to pay attention to what's going on inside of me, when I look closely at my thoughts and actions instead of ignoring them. When I observe myself in this way, I can begin to see how I am unwittingly harmful, how I beat myself, and how I hate myself for being harmful. And once I've seen these things, it's possible to stop doing them. Being less harmful to myself causes me to be gentler, kinder, and more compassionate with others as well, and I begin to relate to them in less violent ways.

To open our eyes and hearts is painful. There is a great deal of pain in seeing life as it truly is. And there is a great deal less suffering. The suffering happens when we try to turn away, when we attempt to remain ignorant and pretend that we are not doing what we are doing and not allowing what we are in fact encouraging and supporting. And the reason that there is so much suffering is that, in order not to feel and not to care what happens to others, we must turn away from our heart, from our true nature, and at the deepest level, from ourselves.

There Is Nothing Wrong With You
An Extraordinary Eight-Day Retreat
based on the book
There Is Nothing Wrong With You: Going Beyond Self-Hate
by Cheri Huber

Inside each of us is a "persistent voice of discontent." It is constantly critical of life, the world, and almost everything we say and do. As children, in order to survive, we learned to listen to this voice and believe what it says.

This retreat, held at the beautiful Zen Monastery Practice Center near Murphys, California, in the western foothills of the Sierra Nevada, is eight days of looking directly at how we have been rejecting and punishing ourselves and discovering how to let that go. Through a variety of exercises and periods of group processing, participants will gain a clearer perspective on how they live their lives and on how to find compassion for themselves and others.

This work is challenging, joyous, fulfilling, scary, courageous, demanding, freeing, loving, kind, and compassionate—compassionate toward yourself and everyone you will ever know.

For information on attending, contact:
Zen Monastery Practice Center
P.O. Box 1979
Murphys, CA 95247
Ph.: 209-728-0860
Fax: 209-728-0861
Email: zencentr@volcano.net

How to order books by American Zen teacher
Cheri Huber

Available from your local bookstore or order in the following ways:
Call toll-free 1-800-337-3040. Fax order to 1-209-728-0861.
To order by mail, send order and payment to the address below.
Visa, Mastercard and Discover card accepted.

____	There Is Nothing Wrong With You*	0-9636255-0-0	$12.00
____	How You Do Anything Is How You Do Everything: A Workbook	0-9636255-5-1	$10.00
____	The Depression Book*	0-9636255-6-X	$12.00
____	The Fear Book*	0-9636255-1-9	$10.00
____	Be the Person You Want to Find*	0-9636255-2-7	$12.00
____	The Key and the Name of the Key Is Willingness*	0-9636255-4-3	$10.00
____	Nothing Happens Next	0-9636255-3-5	$8.00
____	Sex and Money: A Guided Journal	0-9636255-7-9	$12.00
____	Suffering Is Optional	0-9636255-8-6	$12.00
____	That Which You Are Seeking Is Causing You To Seek*	0-9614754-6-3	$10.00
____	Time-Out for Parents*	0-9614754-4-7	$12.00
____	The Monastery Cookbook		$16.00

*Also available as a book on tape. Call for prices.
Books and tapes also sold in discounted sets. Call for prices and a catalog.

Name: _____

Address _____

City· _____ State _____ Zip _____

Please send the books I have checked above $ _____

Postage and Handling: $3 each book, $1 for each add'l book $ _____

7.25% Sales Tax (California residents only) $ _____

                              TOTAL ENCLOSED $ _____

If ordering by mail and using a credit card, send card number and expiration
date to: KEEP IT SIMPLE, P.O. BOX 1979, MURPHYS, CA 95247

Orders out of U.S. send double postage. Overpayments will be refunded. A
complete catalog will be sent with your order.

Zen Monastery Practice Center
P.O. Box 1979
Murphys, CA 95247

Telephone: 209-728-0860

Fax: 209-728-0861

Email: zencentr@volcano.net

Website: www.keepitsimple.org

For a one-year subscription to the Center's quarterly newsletter and calendar of events, *In Our Practice*, send a check for $12.00 along with your name and address.